Blue Ridge Christmas

By Chrissie Anderson Peters

CAP Publishing

Bristol, TN

Blue Ridge Christmas

Copyright Pending ©2019 Chrissie Anderson Peters

CAP Publishing

284 Midway Dr.

Bristol, TN 37620

This book is comprised of stories based on the author's memories. Those memories may differ from the memories of others involved, but are set down as they are for the sake of art and telling specific stories. No malicious or falsified comments are intended by the author.

Book cover designed by Tammy Mays Adams; book cover art copyright ©2019 Tammy Mays Adams.

Printed in the United States of America

ISBN-13: 978-0-9852574-2-2

Blue Ridge Christmas

By Chrissie Anderson Peters

CAP Publishing

Other Books By the Author

Dog Days and Dragonflies (2012)

Running From Crazy (2013)

This book is dedicated to the memory of my Papaw, Arthur James Little, and his love and gift of storytelling, without which I would not be who I am…

And to "My People," everywhere you happen to be on this great big Planet Earth!

Advance Praise for Blue Ridge Christmas

"Chrissie Anderson Peters captures the spirit of the season with these wonderful tales that embrace family and the Appalachia she loves. Chrissie shows us how things that change our lives can happen on an icy Christmas morning with a newborn billy goat or standing in line at the post office. Her belief in a shared humanity shines through in "Mary Kay Christmas" and "My People," but most of all, her tales pay tribute to those she loves and those she now spends Christmas with only in her memories." -- Rebecca Elswick, author of *Mama's Shoes*

~ ~ ~

"Chrissie Anderson Peters brings a tremendous amount of warmth and authenticity to her memories, such as how a single video suddenly launched her into Duran Duran devotion. Chrissie's voice resonates throughout the book, inviting readers to join in on her reflection, and the journey is a pleasure to embark on." -- Andrew "Durandy" Golub, author of *Beautiful Colors* and *The Music Between Us*

~ ~ ~

"Again and again, Chrissie Anderson Peters reminds us about everything that's magical, revealing the true spirit of Christmas." -- Denton Loving, author of *Crimes Against Birds*

~ ~ ~

~ ~ ~

Christmas Tales

*Denotes republication; originally published in *Clinch Mountain Review*, 2018

Virginia Creeper Christmas

My Papaw Little told lots of stories, often over and over and many of them left me wanting to know more. The story of the Virginia Creeper train handing out Christmas gifts, for example. When he first told me the story, I asked, "The Santa Train came into Ashe County?"

"No, it was just a train. They hauled everything on it, supplies, lumber, people. It ran all the time, but at Christmas, they dropped off gifts. Wasn't no Santa Claus involved."

Again, convinced that I was going to correct and expand his memories, I said, "Yeah, it goes down through Kingsport and over into Kentucky and drops off presents at Christmas time."

"No, it ran from Abingdon, down through Grayson and Ashe. They called it the Virginia Creeper because it crept up the mountains so slow."

I had never heard of anything except for "The Santa Train" doing something like this, and part of me wondered if he was just confused. But his memory of getting those presents were quite clear to him, even if I had doubts.

So, here's the scoop. "The Santa Train" started in 1942 and has grown into such a spectacle that it still takes place annually, but now with a celebrity aboard, and Santa Claus to hand out toys at various stops. It runs from Pikeville, Kentucky, to Kingsport, Tennessee. According to their Facebook page, the Santa Train makes 14 stops in Kentucky, Virginia, and Tennessee, giving out in excess of $300,000 in toys, clothing, food, etc. In 2019, it will take its 77th holiday expedition the Saturday before Thanksgiving. It has sponsorship from several major corporations.

But in Ashe County, North Carolina, there is an almost-forgotten tradition of a similar nature, one that would have started two decades before the Santa Train began its work. *The Virginia Creeper in Ashe County* by the Ashe County Historical Society, published in 2011, and tells stories and provides pictorial evidence and information about the Virginia Creeper train's tracks finally came from Virginia, across the North Carolina border in 1914. It ceased to run in 1977, when the

Abingdon line was abandoned. Like the current Santa Train, the Virginia Creeper, in its heyday, sported 14 actual stops. However, it was also known to stop and pick up passengers or to make deliveries to rural residents in between the designated depots. No Christmas stories exist in this book, nor did I find any online, which seems to me to make this little tale all the more important to include in this collection of stories.

The way Papaw told it, it was just someone on the train -- one of the employees -- who distributed gifts. And "distributed" isn't exactly how it sounds. There were no stops. The train would slow and the man would lower presents tied to ropes off the back of the train. The children would chase after the train to get the gifts. Like the Santa Train, these gifts reached some of the poorest rural communities in the region.

I asked Papaw on several occasions what kinds of toys they got. "Nothing big, but it sure seemed like the world to us at the time." Papaw was born in Ashe County in 1924, and had moved to Tazewell, Virginia by 1930. So this was when he was a very young boy.

He also recalled someone they called "The Candy Man," another employee who frequently stood at the back of the train and threw candy off for the kids. Seeing the train go by was always a highlight in those early times, so there was almost always someone standing at the crossings or waiting at the depots along the route. It's hard for me to imagine growing up in those days, waiting for trains being a highlight of youth, hoping to get some candy, and thankful that someone, somewhere was able to send those Christmas gifts across the mountains to be given away like that. I believe that story deserves to live on, even though the train ceased operations decades ago. Like those presents, the stories have become what is so special and should continue to be told. And so it is with this collection of tales from the Blue Ridge Mountains.

Papaw and Santa Claus

The first Christmas that I remember was probably my third. We had moved from the single-wide trailer where my Aunt Susan, Mom, and I lived with Mamaw and Papaw, to the double-wide where we lived with them on the same lot of land. I think it was even our first Christmas in the double-wide, but the same year that Papaw had retired from Ford Motor Company in Detroit and stopped driving back and forth between Michigan and Virginia all the time.

So, Christmas of 1974, I was antsy and excited. Santa came to see me on Christmas Eve -- that's how he does it, you know. Some kids get their presents on Christmas Eve so that he's all finished by Christmas morning. And, since my last name was Anderson, when I was a little older, I reasoned that he must go alphabetically. (No wonder I grew up to be a librarian, with logic like that!)

Papaw kept trying to do stuff in the back bedroom and coming out for different tools, then locking the door behind him when he went back in. My Papaw's nickname for me was Chrissle-the-Gristle, growing up. "Now, Chrissle, you stay away from that door!

Papaw's busy back there and I don't want you in the middle of everything!"

Finally, I heard him say to Mamaw, "Dot, you's gotta get her out of here for a while. Go driving around." And thus began a long-standing Christmas Eve tradition that lasted most of my adolescence. We got in the car -- Susan, Mamaw, Mom, and me -- and we just aimlessly drove around, looking at Christmas lights. I remember in Adria, way up on the hill, below Adria Advent Christian Church, there was a light-up manger scene. We pulled over into the driveway at Granny Vance's sister Leo's house so I could see it better. I loved it! That manger scene continued to adorn that hillside past the time that I lived in Tazewell, and I left in 1995 to move to Roanoke.

We drove partway up Baptist Valley. I oooh'd and ahhh'd over everything. Light-up Santas, snowmen, choir children. All of the lights just seemed like magic.

Our church, Yost Chapel Freewill Baptist, was further down the Valley, right beside the turn-off for The Jumps and shortly before the turn-off to Cochran Hollow (Cochern Holler, as the locals call it). The church had already had their Christmas play. We did not have *pageants*, and I had been in the angel choir *and* had a part to say, which I still remember to this day: "A little heart all cleansed from sin, for I have let the Savior in." (Yes, I really do remember all of this this vividly from the age of three.) We turned around at Yost Chapel, and I heard Mom whisper to Mamaw, "You think he's had enough time?"

I remember thinking, "Oh, they took me out so I wouldn't see Santa!" I was a little disappointed, but also very excited to see if he thought I'd been a good girl.

Mamaw looked at her watch and said, "Yeah, just drive home slow."

We got home around 8:00 p.m. This is the reason that I always opened gifts at 8:00 p.m. from that Christmas Eve forward. This one Christmas set the mood for every Christmas after except for two, each of Mom's subsequent marriages managing to louse up one for various reasons.

I ran into the house, and there was Papaw, reclined on the floor beside the Christmas tree. "Well, Chrissle, you just missed him by a few minutes! But he sure did leave you a lot of presents!"

And he had. That was the year that I got a chalkboard and bench so I could draw -- I scribbled way more than I drew -- even then, God was giving me words, not pictures. And a "baby" baby grand piano from Jayco. It was solid white and I banged and banged on it! I loved music already. And there she was, my very own big baby doll, with my same name, Baby Crissy. I remember that she spelled her name differently, but she was beautiful! Auburn red hair that you could pull out to give her hair the illusion of "growing" long enough for a ponytail in the back. She was wearing a cute pink outfit and had the prettiest brown eyes, with big, thick, fake eyelashes (which one of my cousins later pulled out, the heathen).

Once all of the excitement had calmed down, I took Baby Crissy over to Papaw, who was eating a slice of Mamaw's applesauce cake, one of my most favorite things that she ever made. He pretended to give her a bite, and I took a bite. I hugged him and said, "I'm glad you got to see Santa." And he hugged me back, looking tired, but happy.

Do They Know It's Christmas?

I remember it vividly. Friday night, 30 November 1984. I was spending the night with my best friend Pam, who had just turned twelve that week and recently gotten braces. I was a year ahead of her in school and had turned thirteen in August. The local news went off at 11:35 and we eagerly awaited the main event of our sleepover: Friday Night Videos!

MTV was a dream to some of us who lived so far out in the sticks that cable didn't even reach us yet in 1984. So we got our video fixes each Friday night from 11:35-12:35 with Friday Night Videos. There were occasional guest spots by our favorite rockers, usually just long enough to introduce the next song. Which was fine. The more videos, the better!

Let me start this by saying that I knew full-well who Duran Duran were. I even knew some of their music and enjoyed it. I had watched some of the videos and -- how did they make that water come falling out of the big screen during "The Reflex?" But that was as far as it went. Every girl I knew was gaga over the band, but I had vowed to stay my course and remain true to Michael Jackson. But this was the night that changed it all.

First up that night was Band-Aid, a group of British mega-stars joining forces to sing a song to help raise money for starving people in Africa. The project was spear-headed by Bob Geldof, of a group called The Boomtown Rats. I sat down to watch the video, as Pam stood there, carefully brushing her braces.

"At Christmastime, there's no need to be afraid." Ooooh, dreamy Paul Young. And thus began the excitement of seeing who's who in the video.

"But say a prayer, and pray for the other ones," George Michael cooed.

"At Christmastime, it's hard, but when you're having fun/ There's a world outside your window…"

Stop the presses! "Pam, Pam! Who is that guy?" I asked in reference to the hot blonde with the scruffy face who had just sung those lines.

Still brushing her braces, she answered, "Um, I think that's Simon LeBon. He's the lead singer of Duran Duran."

Mental note to myself: I might need to check out Duran Duran a little more.

Throughout the video, they kept flashing this beautiful -- and I *do* mean *beautiful* man -- with flawless make-up, but never stayed on his image long enough that Pam could tell me who he was.

Then there was this guy wearing a Duran Duran sweatshirt. "Let me guess," I said sarcastically, "he's in Duran Duran, too?"

"Yeah, I think he plays guitar," she said. "Maybe bass. His name is John. John Taylor, maybe? It's really weird, like three of them have the same last name."

And finally, towards the end, they panned to *that* face, and I said, "Oh, my gosh, Pam! *Who is he?*"

Still brushing her braces meticulously, she answered, "Oh, he's in Duran Duran, too. He plays keyboards. I think his name is Nick Rhodes."

"How many people are in Duran Duran?" I asked.

"Five. Then she pointed out Roger Taylor and Andy Taylor in the group lineup at the end, where everyone is singing, "Feed the world, let them know it's Christmastime…""

Five. I had just randomly picked out three -- yeah, I'd count the guy wearing the sweatshirt as random -- guys from this video of dozens and they were all in Duran Duran. That definitely merited further investigation. Then came the first commercial break, with the promise of Duran Duran's new video, "Wild Boys" up next.

Pam had finished brushing her braces and we sat down on the couch, eagerly awaiting the return of FNV.

And that's when the deal was sealed! Simon, the rough-looking blonde rogue appeared on the screen strapped to a wheel, and I shrieked aloud in delight. "Oh. My. Lord!" I threw myself off the couch and closer to the TV set. "Look at him, just *look* at him, Pam!"

From down the hall, her dad called out a warning, "Girls, quiet down!"

The whole video just gave me an indescribable rush! This was teenage lust at its finest! Five of them, I kept thinking! Five of them!!! There was only one Michael Jackson. And from that moment he was history, as I began collecting a lifetime of memorabilia that still exists in part today, thirty-five years later.

One of the highlights of my life was getting to do a Skype with John Taylor, bassist of Duran Duran, as the result of winning a celebrity auction just before Christmas in 2013 through a really amazing charity called Road Recovery. (A quick bit about Road Recovery, just because, if you're reading this and don't know about them, you should! Road Recovery helps at-risk teens and young adults battling addiction and other adversities through the efforts of entertainment industry professionals who have confronted similar issues and now wish to share the experience, knowledge, and resources by collaborating with them to create and present live-concert events and studio recording projects.)

John is quite involved with Road Recovery, and during the Skype, one of the things I told him was how I became a Duranie (that's what the "tribe" of fans calls ourselves, by the way). I remember him saying to me, "How odd! You may be the only person in the world to start liking us over a song that wasn't even Duran Duran." I laughed. And I relayed this entire story to him, including the part about the guy wearing the Duran Duran sweatshirt. He placed his hand over his face and shook his head, "Can you believe that I was actually that cheesy???"

And there I sat, in a study room at the community college library where I worked, laughing with that guy from that video, twenty-nine years after the fact. Truly. Laughing. Holding my own in an actual conversation, with no drooling or schoolgirl giggling.

Cheesy? Sure, but give me cheese, and happiness, and giddiness any day over disillusionment and heartbreak. All those years, and I was still screaming during those songs. I was still a crazy fan whose life had been saved many times over because of the music of that band. I was part of a community that not only understood that mix of emotions, but echoed them back in volume. All because of a great humanitarian effort that brought the world together for a cause that ignited my passion for a band of Wild Boys from Birmingham.

Zat You, Squeaky Fromme?

I was 13 when my sister Sarah was born. I've always referred to her as my sister, and, even though we had different fathers, we lived and grew up in the same place. She called me "Sissy-Mommy" until the week she started kindergarten and I started college. Siblings tend to have "special" relationships, anyway; add to that my mischievousness, and you had a Christmas to remember.

It was December 1987. We had uninstalled the fireplace that came in our double wide in favor of a wood-/coal-burning stove, so there was no fireplace for Santa to come down that year. I already had my plans for Christmas Eve laid out in my head.

Sarah was three that year, so I was 16. Two years earlier, her father, Tom, had decided that Sarah, because she was his child, would open her gifts on Christmas morning, just like he had as a child. One problem. I opened my gifts, and always had, on Christmas Eve. That first Christmas, I refused to open any of the presents under the tree on Christmas morning except my boom box. I could be a little stubborn, cantankerous -- and I was a teenager whose annual routine for the biggest holiday of the year had just been jerked out from underneath her for a kid who didn't even understand Christmas yet.

By 1986, the year before this story, we had come to a compromise. I could open all of my gifts except one on Christmas Eve, and then one on Christmas morning when Sarah opened hers from Santa. Whichever one I opened just had to say "From Santa." Likewise, she could open a few presents from family on Christmas Eve when I opened my gifts, sharply at 8 p.m., with Mamaw and Papaw Little there to watch, as they always had, and then Santa's gifts were her big surprise on Christmas morning. As long as I got to keep my tradition, I was fine with the arrangement. She was new; she didn't know any better or even care. She was a kid. You could give her a big, empty box and she could occupy herself for hours on end with that!

But in 1987, the fireplace was gone. Sarah was fighting sleep in a big way that night. She was still wide awake when the 11:00 news report came on, proclaiming that Squeaky Fromme was still at large after her daring escape from the federal women's prison in nearby Alderson, West Virginia. Squeaky had been missing since the 23rd. For those of you who may be unfamiliar with Squeaky, (real name Lynette), she was one of Charles Manson's most faithful followers, and had attempted to assassinate President Gerald Ford. Either one of those factors was likely to land you in trouble, but both was a certain prison sentence.

It was sleeting outside that night, and I started thinking about how cold and miserable Squeaky must be, out there on the run. The sleet made a sizzling sound against the stovepipe that came down through the roof into the stove. I turned from the television and looked over at precious little Sarah, wanting to wait to see Santa come. And I was typically not mean to her at all. Why I chose Christmas to do so is still beyond me, really. But the words came tumbling out of my mouth, with a smile on my face.

"Hey, Sarah. How's Santa gonna get in here tonight to bring your presents?" She did a double-take, looked over at the stove, and said, "Him come down the chimbly." As children, we were taught that the thing smoke left a fireplace from was called a chimbly, or a chimly. I don't know that I knew the proper word -- chimney -- until late elementary school.

"Ya think so? I mean, he can get down there, but then what? There's no handle on the door on the inside of the stove so he can let himself out. What if he just burns up in there?"

Oh, she was wide awake now! And my mother was shooting glances at me that I knew had words and soon-to-be actions behind them. "Sarah," she said sternly, more to me than to Sarah, "you tell your sissy that he doesn't need a handle. He's magical."

"Yeah, Sissy, him's magic!"

Still, she sat there another 90 minutes, dozing off, and then waking up to the sound of the sleet, commencing to worry about Santa all over again. I knew that I was in trouble. I'd probably get grounded or lose my allowance but, somehow, it felt okay. I was always good to the kid. She'd wake up the next morning, Santa would have brought her gifts and gone on his merry way again, so she would know that he escaped the fiery furnace. It made me giggle inside.

Once Mom finally got her put down for the night, she let into me with a lecture about scaring Sarah and how horrible I was. I apologized halfheartedly, and went to my own room around 2 a.m. I got up once and went to the kitchen to get a glass of milk. Tom, my stepfather, was assembling a miniature John Deere tractor for Sarah. You pedaled it like a bike which, of course, she could not do at the age of three, but she pushed that thing all over the hillside of the God-Forsaken Hill until she learned. (I had affectionately termed Tom's property the "God-Forsaken Hill" the first time I saw it, as it was so far away from the main road, and up very rugged terrain that most people wouldn't even try to drive up it in their vehicles, cutting me off from civilization.)

"How's it going?" I asked.

"A lot harder than it looked, but I'm about finished." He took a sip of coffee -- as a retired truck driver, he was rarely without a cup of coffee at hand -- and looked at me over the top of his glasses that had slid down to the tip of his nose. "You know, they said they thought that they spotted that woman in Tazewell on the last update."

"Squeaky? They spotted Squeaky somewhere here in Tazewell???"

"That's what they said." Then he sipped his coffee and went back to work on Sarah's tractor.

I finished my glass of milk and put my glass in the sink before returning to my bedroom. My bed was situated along the wall where the windows were and they were not terribly high off the ground. I could climb in and out of my bedroom window easily by using the porch, and had done so many times. Squeaky in Tazewell. On the lam. And we lived on the secluded God-Forsaken Hill. I could be murdered in my sleep and no one would ever know. Tom would probably just invite her in for coffee; he never met a stranger. For the next few hours, I lay there with the covers pulled up tight around me, occasionally looking out, when I thought that I heard someone messing with the window, but it was only the sleet.

When Sarah woke up to open her presents, I rushed out of my bedroom to join her -- to join anyone -- in some room other than mine. Mom looked at me with a half-grin. "You look pretty rough this morning."

"Yeah," I said lamely. "I guess I was just excited."

"You didn't think that Squeaky was getting in if Santa couldn't, did you?" she smirked and looked over at Tom, who had a great big laugh at my expense.

I went in and hugged Sarah. "I'm sorry I was mean to you last night about Santa."

She was already puttering around the living room on her tractor. "I told you him was magic!"

Chrissie Had a Little Goat

When I grew up and left home, going back always made me feel like I had something to prove, something to show for my efforts of "getting out." Mom often accused me of "getting above my raising," which I suppose was how I acted sometimes. But it was only because I wanted everyone to see that I was doing well for myself, to see that I was making it just fine for a single girl in this big world.

And that was another point of contention. I was twenty-nine years old and not a grandchild in sight. That's how things worked where I was from. Typically, you married young and, by the time you were my age, you had at least a couple of half-grown kids. I'd brought a few guys home, mostly ones I met online -- this was 2000, way before eHarmony and ChristianMingle -- and one I had even thought might be the one. Until his Italian parents met me, and then I knew that all hope was gone. (This is a story still referred to as "The Thanksgiving of Angry Italians" -- another story for another time.)

It irked me to no end that my mother still thought that getting married and birthing babies was going to be my destiny! I had a *career*. I was a *professional librarian*. I had a *future in my field*. I was *doing more* than living paycheck to paycheck. And I was *having fun* flirting online! Why couldn't she just be proud of me and stop wanting grandchildren?

I was dating a guy online named Russ. He was from Chicago, but was living in Austin. This seemed to appease her enough to get through the Christmas meal without too much harassment.

When we got back to her house on the God-Forsaken Hill, I put on my new leopard-print pajamas from Lane Bryant to show to her. (It was the 90's -- everything was animal print.) They were so soft and luxurious, perfect for a freezing winter night like that night. It had started snowing during dinner and hadn't stopped, which was kinda exciting. Snow for Christmas. But it also meant that I was probably going to be stuck on the God-Forsaken Hill for an extra day or two. She lovingly touched the pajamas, appreciating them, and then turned on a dime. "And how much did *those* cost you?"

Normally, I wouldn't have given the actual price. I didn't like to make Mom feel bad about money. I knew that she and Tom had it pretty tight sometimes. But she had asked so nastily that I spat the amount at her, and then retreated to my old bedroom to call Russ long-distance.

Back then, long-distance phone calls were a big deal -- they cost money, and depending on the day or time of day, could be expensive. And international calls? Whoa! You could blow an entire paycheck on those -- or so, I had heard. Wink-wink! There was no answer, so I came back out after a while and put the phone up. It amazed me that they still had that same extension cord on it that had been placed on there when I was a teenager, so they could monitor where the phone was when I talked on it and for how long.

Tom was quite a bit older than Mom and Mom was twenty years older than me. Which, that Christmas meant that she was forty-nine, and he was seventy-four. He would go outside on the farm and work himself half to death. In the summer, it was the hay fields and keeping the tractor in good repair. In the winter, it was pushing snow off of parking lots up town and trying to look after the livestock. Living on a farm was never easy. Being a true farmer was to be admired, but was nothing that I never wanted any part of. No vacations. No days off, really. And a lot of literal blood, sweat, and tears for not a whole lot in return.

He had been outside longer than we knew he should have been, and Mom started to get dressed to go find him. I stopped her -- Mom was not in the greatest of health herself. "You are *not* going out in that snow, Mother!" I admonished. "I'll get dressed and go look for him. Just find me a good flashlight."

Just as I turned to go change clothes, Tom came to the door, soaking wet with sweat, holding something in his arms. Mom pushed me aside and said, "Oh, Lord, what is it?"

"It's a goat, a baby goat. The mama left it in the snow and took the other one. I can't tell if it's even breathing, Dora."

Mom found a box to put the goat in and grabbed a couple of towels from her bathroom. They sat it by the stove to get as much heat to it as possible.

"What can I do?" I asked. I, of no maternal instincts or interests. But it was clearly dead or going to die unless some sort of miracle occurred.

Tom looked at my fancy pajamas. "Nah, nah, you'll get them fancy pajamas all messed up."

Now it was a challenge. "Tell me what to do until you can warm up and take over."

He peered at me again over his frosted glasses. "Well, if you take this towel and just rub it as hard as you can. I don't even know for sure that it's alive. I found it out in the snow by itself. She had one and they almost always had two, so I just kept looking and found him way out…"

I'd moved to the floor and commenced rubbing the poor little thing with the threadbare towel. I made a mental note to find a reason to buy Mom some better towels soon. Tom went to change clothes and try to find a bottle that he could mix formula in to feed the goat if he came around.

I was getting nowhere with this towel in a box thing. And before I realized what had happened, I'd lifted the stiff-limbed kid out of the box and settled in on the sofa and pulled him in as close to my body as I could, figuring that the heat from my body, along with the rubbing of the towel might do something. He lay there, absolutely still, me willing him to move. Nothing. A good ten minutes went by and I realized that I was praying to God for this little guy to be alive, to be okay.

Tom came in and offered to take him from me. "No," I said, "I feel like I'm making progress."

"You're ruining those pajamas. Them look like they cost a lot."

"Doesn't matter," I replied. "They'll wash." I looked down and they sure enough were a mess. I had afterbirth all over me. The ice that was matted to his little body had melted and I was soaking wet, but it was a warm wet. I asked Tom to hand me the other towel. I resumed rubbing, small soothing circles, and talking softly to him. I don't even know what I was saying. I doubt that I knew then. I just wanted him to realize that there was someone there who cared about him, someone who wanted him to pull through.

About that time, his eyes flashed open, his tongue stuck out, and he kicked real hard. I was scared to death. I thought that he was going into convulsions or something horrible like that!

Tom leaned forward in his chair. "Keep going! Keep going! He's breathing now, he's coming around!" He got up to get the soda bottle with a black nipple affixed to it. "Here, let me have him. I'll see if he'll eat."

"I guess we've come this far together," I said. "Hand me the bottle and I'll see if he'll eat."

"Now this nipple ain't the best. It'll get all over you."

"Please, I've got afterbirth and probably worse than that on me right now. Hand me the bottle. I'm bringing this little guy home."

Much to my surprise, he took the bottle greedily, starving as I'm sure he was. His brown eyes glistening as he tugged mightily at the bottle. I remember thinking that I was glad I wasn't a nanny goat, 'cos that would have to hurt. Once he ate a little, I finished rubbing him, end to end, over and under. And

I just held him close to me. He was so soft. Softer than those silly pajamas. Tom asked for him back and I went ahead, happily hearing him bleat throughout the house.

I asked Mom if she had a gown or pajamas or something that I could change into while I washed my clothes. "Nothing as nice as yours," she retorted.

"I just need something I can wear while these are washing, Mom. And if you have any darks, throw them over here. I'll just wash them all together."

As I put the laundry in and tried to decide between smiling and crying, and thanked God for this Christmas miracle, I heard Tom yell at me.

"Chrissie, what are you gonna name him?"

"Is it definitely a him?"

"Yeah, it's a billy!"

I only paused a moment before saying "Jacob." *Jacob have I loved.*

Mary Kay Christmas

When I started selling Mary Kay in 2014, it was completely as a hobby. Just a way to help us make some extra money to put a new roof on the house. By 2015, I was really into it, winning cool quarterly prizes, building a team all over the country. I was on fire!

In any sort of retail, the last quarter of the year is huge. Companies pull out all the stops for the holidays so that their customers will do the same, and Mary Kay is no exception. So I sat down with my Director and strategized how to best capitalize on the Christmas season in Mary Kay. We had a plan. My sales were going to be through the roof, and it would be a great Christmas season for me!

The whole "Big Team," which consisted of five Directors and all of their team members, announced that they were adopting a nursing home in Lebanon, Virginia, to take Mary Kay gifts to a lip balm and a small bottle of lotion for each of the fifty residents. I was so moved by that and started figuring out how many I could contribute.

Then I derailed from the planned route that I had made with my Director. Actually, I didn't derail; God put me on a whole different set of tracks. Not a path one of luxurious colognes, or one that focused on glitzy holiday colors, or one that targeted special gift-sized or repackaged favorites.

As I drove to do deliveries one day, God said, "You're gonna do that, too. You're going to give to those who need love, those who don't have loved ones or friends to share the holidays with, just like the Big Team. But you're going to do more than that. I want you to do Heritage Hall in Tazewell."

"But God, they've already picked the nursing home they're going to help."

"And I've picked the one that you're going to help. Heritage Hall in Tazewell." I didn't know the exact number, but I knew that Heritage Hall had way more than fifty patients.

The nursing home that the whole "Big Team" was helping had fewer than fifty patients; and there were a lot more than fifty people on the Big Team. But God wanted me to do Heritage Hall, in my hometown of Tazewell, all by myself. I believe in God; I trust in God; but I also wondered what God was thinking? I couldn't do that by myself!

But I went home and called Heritage Hall, anyway. If I was going to argue with God, I at least needed to know my statistics Heritage Hall has three sections -- assisted living, rehabilitation, and long-term care. About 50 patients in each. "Whoa, God! The Big Team is doing like fifty all together and *you* want *me* to do three times that amount on my own? How fair is that?"

"You won't do it alone. Others will help."

And that was the end of that, although I felt more than a little like Noah being told to build an ark. How could I be expected to do this alone? And why me? Still, if he was going to send someone to help me accomplish the task, I'd move forward.

Okay, so I know a little bit about fundraising. I'd done some in college with our sorority. I'd certainly done a lot of it in my work in public libraries over the years. In fact, I couldn't think of any job I'd ever had that didn't involve some sort of fundraising. And that was when it hit me. The community. Surely there were businesses and organizations in Tazewell that would be willing to help with a project like this. I could think of five or six who could easily underwrite such a project. So I placed my Mary Kay order for 175 lip balms, and 175 full-sized hand creams. Gender-friendly. Anyone could use lip balm and hand cream! The total came to roughly $1750. And I started making my phone calls.

"No, we give in other ways."

"Who are you? I don't recognize your name."

"Which organization are you with?"

"I'm pretty sure that other people do things for the residents there."

But no, no one did anything for *all* of the residents at Heritage Hall. I had asked specifically. Yes, there were churches and other groups that did things for *some* residents, but *not all* of them. After all, doing something for 150 people was an expensive endeavor. At any rate, it became clear very quickly that I was getting nowhere as a lone agent on this mission, and it was more than frustrating.

When the two huge boxes of Mary Kay items arrived, my husband looked at me. I had told him that God wanted me to help the residents of Heritage Hall, and what God told me that he wanted me to do. Russ didn't grow up in church like I did -- every time the doors were open, you were there, whether you wanted to be or not. Russ was more than a little skeptical about this whole thing. What he saw was two big boxes, which I quickly emptied over into one to try to make it look better, and the knowledge that I had just put a whole lot of Mary Kay product on my credit card. And thus far, no businesses in my hometown were willing to help underwrite the project.

The boxes arrived in October. That month passed and the box just sat there at the top of the stairs. Every time Russ walked by it, he just stopped, looked into it, and shook his head. I kept praying for an answer, but nothing was revealed to me in any dramatic way -- no burning bush, no rainbow, no ram to keep from sacrificing someone. I was beginning to feel really stupid. Maybe it wasn't God. Maybe I just wanted to outshine the Big Team. No, I knew that wasn't true! I had to put the doubt behind me and just trust in him. He said that others would help, and they would!

By the time November rolled around, Russ started asking, "God said that other people were going to help you. When is that gonna start happening?" That box of unused, unpaid for product really was like my very own ark.

"He'll supply all my needs," I'd call back. And to myself, I'd add, "Yes, I sure hope so!"

Feeling the disappointment and worry that emanated from Russ every time he looked at that box and questioned my conversation with God was overwhelming on many levels. Financially, $1750 was a huge amount to be stuck with, especially when it is all two very specific products. Spiritually, it was difficult for me to try to explain my faith. And maritally, it was simply gutting not to feel like we were on the same page.

When we went to Chicago for Thanksgiving, I told Russ' mom and his sister Elise about the project. They, too, thought that I was a little crazy, but that the idea behind the insanity was noble. I had told Russ that, if I got it all paid for from donations, I wanted him to play Santa Claus and deliver the items with me. He had kinda laughed and said, "Sure, I'll do that."

When we got back home, I had a serious talk with God. "Okay, you told me to do this. I stepped out on faith and spent $1750 to get these products. You promised that I would not be in this alone. I trust you, but I need for you to show me how this is going to happen. I have less than a month until Christmas, God. Please, give me a sign!"

My Facebook account dinged, notifying me of a message. Was this my sign? Facebook? Should I post on Facebook, and some business would mysteriously say, "We changed our mind, can we help?"

So I wrote a post on Facebook, explaining the purpose of the project, the cost, and how I was doing all of this at my Mary Kay wholesale cost, so I was making no money from it whatsoever. But that God had led me to do this and that I felt like these folks, many who never got visits from family or friends, deserved a little bit of extra cheer at Christmas.

I'm part of several groups, some focusing on genealogy, some from college, some from high school, and one that is a fan community for the British band, Duran Duran. We're called Duranies. Almost immediately after I made my post, a Duranie friend, from New York said, "Hey, I can give you $10 for a set?" And another friend from Hawaii did the same. Soon, Duranies from all over were donating money. And friends from my college days. What surprised me was the lack of people from my hometown. This was for *their* community.

Then a friend I'd gone to church with as a teenager messaged me with a very generous donation -- he had left Tazewell County years before. His mother, also no longer living in Tazewell County, also donated. Then a lady from that same church contacted me. She worked in a bank and spread the news to their clients, as well as to others in that church. I hadn't been to that church in years and had moved my membership two decades earlier. I had never even thought of approaching a church. Which, when I thought about it, was absolutely silly. If God tells you something, why not approach a church before businesses?

Most of the gifts came from people who couldn't be with their grandparents for the holidays, or whose grandparents were in nursing homes, and they hoped that someone would do something like this for them. I even got a donation from New Zealand. People everywhere love their grandparents, it turns out. As the money finally started coming in by early December, I wrapped each lotion and lip balm in a holiday bag and put a name tag on it -- from Lynne B., from Shelby B., from Cynthia H., and so on.

Russ stared at me in amazement about halfway through December and said, "You're really going to do this, aren't you?"

"Nah, God's doing the hard part. I'm just talking it up and taking people's money via PayPal and check."

"I guess I better try on the Santa suit," he half-grumbled, half-smiled.

Unbeknownst to me, at Thanksgiving, he had brought back a Santa Claus suit that his mom made for his dad to wear when he used to play Santa Claus for kids. Tears welled up in my eyes. "You *did* believe!"

"I had to. Because you did."

The morning that we were leaving for Tazewell to take everything to Heritage Hall, we were $25 short. Russ smiled, "That can be our contribution." As we left the house, I checked the mail. There were two more checks, one from his mom, that put us over the top! Now I could pay for the bags and ribbons and tags.

My mom went to Heritage Hall with us, and the three of us handed bags out together. We started at the very first room and went to every single room there that day. It took hours! Russ, who is an RN by profession, stopped and talked to everyone who wanted to talk. If someone was sleeping, he gently nudged them awake to let them know that their present had arrived.

Some of my favorite moments were seeing sweet little old ladies' eyes flutter open, and their faces, like children's, turn to looks of sheer surprise and joy. One woman grabbed Russ' hand and whispered, "Oh, Santa! It *is* you! I knew that you would come!"

I was also overwhelmed by how many people tried to find something to give us in return. "No, no," we insisted, "these are from Santa. These are yours to keep."

One woman in a wheelchair, upon receiving her gifts, went wheeling down the hall, proclaiming, "Santa's here, Santa's here! He has presents! Wake up, everyone!"

I saw several people that I knew. Some people that were distant relatives. And I saw my third grade math teacher who, after 35 years, still remembered me. She invited me in to come talk with her. Russ handed out the gifts and went on to the next room. "Well, Chrissie," she started, "tell me what you've done with your life." Talk about a daunting question!

"Well, I went to college at Emory and Henry, was going to be a teacher, but changed my mind. I got my Masters from the University of Tennessee and became a librarian. I've written two books and published them, I've gotten to travel all over the world. I have a wonderful life, Mrs Bowman!"

"And… You married Santa Claus! Not everyone can say that!"

I smiled and said, "No ma'am, they sure can't!" I hugged her and left, feeling like some of my childhood dreams had truly been fulfilled.

All of the nurses and volunteers had to have their pictures made with Santa Claus. Russ, although an introvert, took to it as though he were the real Santa Claus, though. We finally hit the last room. And I cried openly once we had finished and were in the hall. It meant so much to me that Mom had shared the day with us. If we hurried, we could just make it to the Christmas Eve service at Dailey's Chapel, one of the churches back home I'd gone to for years and considered family. Several members of the congregation there had really gotten behind the project and I wanted to be able to deliver a praise report to them, as well as sing some of my old beloved Christmas carols.

Russ and I didn't even exchange Christmas gifts that year. The whole Mary Kay Christmas experience had been gift enough. It renewed my faith in humanity. It brought me closer in my relationship to God.

It made me feel like a kid again, when Christmas was about more than getting. It still stands as one of the two best Christmases of my entire adult life.

Perspective

Life never stands still. It flows in gullies, flooded by our own experiences. If you watch as gullies meet, you will see one of two things. You will see the two gullies combine to become stronger as they go along or you will see one gully consumed by the other. What survives, what you take away, in either case, depends entirely upon you. And your perspective. I remember thinking all of these things as I sat in the post office parking lot, watching little rivulets and gullies and streams of water become one greater rushing of run-off on a particularly rainy day in late November.

A few days earlier would have been my Papaw's 93rd birthday. We had lost him to dementia and Alzheimer's a few years earlier. In the spring. A rather wet May, if I remembered correctly. It occurred to me now that it seemed like an entirely different occurrence when rains came down and flooded streams and low-lying backyards and meadows in the spring than it does when it hammers down on you in the winter. It isn't just about temperature. It isn't just about the time of year or which season it is. It just seems like they are two distant, distinct cousins of the same cumulonimbus beginnings.

The kind of rain falling that day in the post office parking lot was chilling. One of those rains where you got soaked almost immediately and it's cold, so cold that it goes all the way into your bones. I hated that kind of cold. Once you get to that point, it takes forever to warm up again, maybe even a good cup of hot tea with Maker's Mark and honey... Maker's Mark, honey, and tea... That could be a worthwhile reward for being out in all of that nastiness. Such a cold November rain.

I always laughed when I put the words "November" and "rain" into the same sentence, remembering the popular song from my high school days by Guns N Roses. As I sat there, waiting for a break in the downpour, I hummed the chorus and sorta mumbled, "... in the cold November Rain," slipping into my best Axl Rose impersonation. I sighed deeply and decided to make a break for it. If I waited until it slacked off some, the post office would probably already be closed for the day. Those ladies never lingered a moment past

5:00. They couldn't kick you out, as long as you were inside before closing time, but they sure could make you uncomfortable while you were standing there being waited on.

Why was I even *at* the post office? Who even *goes* to the post office, anymore? Well, I did. Nearly every day. I had started playing around with selling things on eBay a few months earlier, selling off my 80's music and memorabilia collection. Business was pretty good right around the holidays. Many friends who dabbled in online sales or business shipping admonished me, "Do you know how much time you're wasting going in there and standing in those ridiculous lines every day? Time is money! You can print off shipping labels at home and just walk right in, drop those puppies of, smile a snarky smile at all those schmucks just standing there doing nothing, while *you* are off to get other things done!"

That was the thing, though. Even if I stood there for thirty minutes -- which had happened on several occasions -- I typically used the post office outings to my advantage. People-watching was a habit. Interacting with strangers -- oh, wait, I never met a stranger --

was something that I found I could experience over and over again later. Kinda like a cow in a summer-green pasture, I could have that experience, take it in slowly, and then regurgitate it later for my own purposes. "Chewing her cud." I heard my Mamaw's voice from somewhere in my childhood. "She's chewing her cud. She has to chew it up real good, that's why she stands there chewing for so long. Then, later, she just throws it up and eats it all over again." I had balked at the very idea of "eating" your own vomit as a child. As an adult, I knew that there were far worse things to have to endure on a daily basis sometimes.

When I got inside, there were a few other people standing in front of me. I became unusually annoyed that everyone had come so unprepared. Couldn't they r*ead* the sign that *clearly* instructed that everything needed to be packaged, addressed, and ready to go when they got to the post office workers? I mean, this was the post office, not Office Depot! My agitation grew as a young mother with a very unhappy baby filed in behind me. *Why* was there only one clerk out front? Anita *was not* a one-woman show! The line was backed up, out into the lobby! Maybe I *did* need to look further into that whole postage labels at home so I could drop and go, I thought.

After what seemed like an eternity, the old woman in front of me slowly made her way to the clerk. She had nothing packaged. She was dropping all these things on the floor and struggling to bend over to retrieve them, losing something else in the process. I took a deep breath. It would be my turn soon. I was next. I only had two things and I was *prepared*, unlike everyone else that afternoon. I drew in my breath and shook my head in indignation.

Once I really started watching the old woman, I realized that she must be a grandmother. I stood silently as she struggled to fit these things into an envelope that she was sending to her grandkids for Christmas. No fancy gifts, I observed. Curly pens. Pencils. Coloring books. Crayons. Even little store-bought bags for the parents to put the gifts into once they arrived. Stuff that probably came from somewhere like a dollar store. In the grand scheme of things, what most people would consider to be "junk." She was trying so hard to stuff all of these little treasures into a regular sized mailer.

Anita patiently tried to stuff it all in there, at least long enough so that she could tape it up. But it wouldn't fit. No amount of professional corralling in the world was gonna get all of this stuff into the undersized manila envelope that the woman had brought for the task at hand. The grandmother looked down at the remaining items in her hands, crest-fallen. "Oh, I guess I'll need to figure out what to leave out." And she started unloading the items, looking at each one. It was as if she weighed every lost reaction in her mind. Which one would be the least disappointing for her grandbabies not to open up on Christmas morning? Which omissions would be less painful?

Somehow, I was the only other person in line. Everyone else had given up and left, and really, who could blame them? The old woman continued to examine each item individually, even going so far as to try to assemble the contents into some mashed up 3-D jigsaw puzzle, clearly traumatized that part of the contents would not be able to make the trip.

I was about to step up to offer to pay. She'd held up a $10 bill, indicating that was all that she had. Anita took a deep breath and smiled at her. "I think we can do *this* for just a couple dollars more." She instructed the grandmother to grab a medium flat-rate box, the side-load variety. She carefully took all of the items from the woman and placed them on the scale. She smiled and said, "There we go. That's gonna be $9.10." The grandmother handed her the $10 bill and thanked her sincerely for packing it all up for her. You could palpably feel the kindness that had just been exchanged in that otherwise tedious and traumatic ten minutes or so.

I flashed back to a memory from childhood that had been filed so deeply that I honestly half-gasped at its resurgence. Every year, my grandparents packed up a huge box for my cousins who lived in Detroit. Their absentee father was my grandparents' son, which I think made it especially important to them that this life-sized box get safely to them each December. I recalled the excitement and care that went into the packing of each box, each year, until I was well into elementary school, when it just became easier to send the kids a check so that they could pick out their own gifts. But for the first few years of my life, the day we packed "the box to go to the kids" was of utmost importance. Everyone in the house joined in to wrap the individual gifts before they made their way into the box. Mamaw, a perfectionist of the utmost order, had to make sure that every Christmas ribbon was placed on just so, annoying the heck out of my Papaw, who frequently retorted, "Dot, just put the stupid bow on there and leave it alone. If it falls off, their mom can put it back on!" He wanted it all to be as "right" as possible, too, but he also knew that he had a deadline and we usually pushed it to the very limit. Finally it was all inside, and then came the truly important part: the packaging. This box would likely go through a lot of bouncing around and jostling before it ever saw Detroit, so the outside packaging was every bit as important as the packaged gifts that went inside. The importance of each strip of brown packing tape still astounds me.

I remember Papaw getting into the car and driving that box all the way to the bus station in Bluefield, because it was cheaper to buy that great big box a *seat* on the Greyhound bus than to mail it through the post office. Rain, snow, sleet, whatever the weather or road conditions, he had to get it to the first stop of its journey before that bus to Detroit left. Every year. And I knew for certain how much that grandmother really did appreciate Anita packing up that box for her. For those grandbabies. And not having a real clue as to what had actually just transpired.

I stood there for a few seconds, fighting back my tears, unable to move forward to complete my own business. Being someone who shipped things and took them to the post office daily, I was pretty familiar with the prices for shipping flat-rate. Flat-rate was one cost: "if it fits, it ships." There was absolutely no reason for Anita to weigh that package, except for the fact that that was what the grandmother *expected* her to do in order to mail it out. That regular sized envelope certainly would have needed to be weighed. The regular size flat rate envelope, which still wouldn't have held the grandmother's items cost $6.65. That middle sized flat-rate box? That one cost $13.60. Not $9.10.

As I stepped up to the counter, the tears just burst out. I bit my lip and tried to compose myself. By now, there were five or six other people in line. I told Anita how much I missed my grandparents, that my Papaw's birthday was a few days before. Our eyes met. Silently, we nodded at each other. When I took out my credit card to pay for my packages, I asked if I could pay the difference on that other package. She just smiled and said, "It's taken care of. I miss my grandparents, too."

My People

On November 28, 2016, devastating wildfires combined with abnormally high winds to create, quite literally, a perfect storm, in the Great Smoky Mountains National Park. In all, nearly 18,000 acres suffered fire damage. A total of 134 people were injured and fourteen people died.

When the winds picked up that night, confusion and chaos ensued. Residents and tourists called 9-1-1, asking if they should evacuate. Was there an actual emergency? The fires seemed to be closing in on homes and blocking roadways. Should people try to leave or stay put? Later, transcripts and tapes of many of those calls were made public, illustrating the complete lack of disaster preparedness. But who could have ever predicted something like this? Emergency services were cut off from entire segments of the area. Some people decided to flee their homes, sometimes with lethal repercussions. Evacuees sat in their cars, in what quickly became a virtual parking lot on the one road out of the town of Gatlinburg, fires on all sides, unable to move forward, unable to go back, unable to find any other way out.

Approximately 1,000 families in Sevier County, Tennessee, completely lost their homes in the fires, some had insurance, but most were without. It was the end of November and Thanksgiving had just passed. The weeks ahead looked bleak. No time was a good time, but the combination of the holidays, colder temperatures as winter set in, the fact that the high tourism season was ended painted a dreary and desolate outlook. Any jobs still existing would be difficult to secure.

One person stepped up to do what no one else, not even entire governmental agencies, would attempt. What no one imagined possible. But this woman knew all about imagination. Decades earlier, she had introduced a program promoting early childhood literacy in Sevier County. In the years since its inception, Imagination Library had grown to include all fifty states and four other countries. Dolly Parton devised a plan. Just hours after the devastation began, Dolly busily contacted her Dollywood Foundation's board members and lawyers, mobilizing troops to help "her people" recover. She announced a concert set for December 2, to help raise funds for survivors who had, in essence, lost everything. The line-up crossed all musical genres and eras. It turned out that when Dolly Parton asked for help, people didn't say no; they just asked what they needed to do. Over $9,000,000 was raised as a direct result of that concert. She pledged to help every single family who could prove residency in the county -- whether *citizenship* was established or not -- and who could provide evidence that their homes were "structurally" uninhabitable. She made sure that the whole world knew, however, that these funds were *not* to be considered a hand-out, but instead "a hand-up."

The Foundation created the system through which residents would apply for and receive $1000 per month, for six consecutive months, to help them get back on their feet. The Foundation, at that time, had only thirteen employees worldwide. The work undertaken seemed immense, but the staff would forge ahead and help those who Dolly still calls "my people."

****

As I listened to the newscasts and watched the live internet feeds the night the fires began, I instinctively knew that I needed to help. I said to my husband, "I need to be there. I have to help." I had just gone through three months of physical therapy for some shoulder issues.

He looked at me in utter disbelief. "You can't go down there. They won't let you in. You're not part of emergency services. And you absolutely cannot volunteer and end up messing up that shoulder again."

He made a valid point. Most volunteer efforts would almost certainly include lifting and moving emergency supplies. Still, I felt a force pulling me to go.

When the "My People Fund" was announced, I seized my opportunity. I had been affiliated with the Imagination Library in my own area for years through my work as a librarian, so I sent an email to the Foundation President. "I don't know if you can use any help, or if you guys have everything covered, but if there is something that I can do, I *really* want to."

He pointed out that it would be a long commute for me, almost two hours each way. "But if you want to help, just be here on Thursday morning at 8."

The first month consisted of intaking applicants, verifying their claims, identities, etc. It would cover four days, each day set up alphabetically by surname. We would operate on Thursday, Friday, Monday, and Tuesday. Through lodging and eating locally, I reasoned that I would support the local economy and truly become a part of the greater community.

I braved the cold December morning and headed for the doors of the LeConte Center. I honestly didn't know what to expect. I knew that I was there to help, but I also knew that this would likely be one of the most difficult things I'd ever faced.

Once inside, I found Daniel, the Foundation President, who greeted me warmly, thanked me for being there, and pointed me to Angel, the Volunteer Coordinator, one of her many functions within the Foundation. Angel smiled, got me signed in, and looked around. "Okay, you're going to be a door greeter. Cathy requested you." I was touched. Cathy was one of the two Regional Managers. I had only met her one time, more than a decade earlier. I was moved that she remembered me, and had asked for me to be her partner at the doors.

The set-up inside the main room was mind-blowingly simple. Eight computer stations lined the exterior walls; volunteers waited eagerly, anxiously, to begin. So many smiling faces. I walked up to Cathy and said, "Angel said that you requested me to help you."

Cathy, who would become a tremendous friend and partner-in-mischief over the next few months, looked at me blankly. "I did?" I laughed. So much for my ego!

On the first of many trips back to Angel's post, I stopped and looked outside. With over an hour until the doors would even open, the line already stretched beyond my line of vision. My heart pounded so hard. I was about to encounter people who had lost everything, sometimes so much more than anything materialistic. And my job was to smile, to welcome them, to do my best to help them.

I watched out the front doors and saw a man walking up and down the line, handing out biscuits from some fast food restaurant. I bit my lip. How incredibly amazing was this community? Some random stranger had taken his time and money to come down and try to make the difficult process better.

As the time approached to begin welcoming people, I looked around. Honestly, it was such a meager operation for such a massive undertaking. How could this possibly be anything but chaos? Just as I started to feel overwhelmed, Daniel called us all together to brief us on what we needed to do and how many people were estimated to come through our doors over the next few days. "When those folks come through those doors, don't just point them to a table and say, 'Just go over to station four.' *You walk them there.* These folks have walked alone in this journey long enough. At least while they're here, we will walk with them."

I looked over at Cathy. Both of us took a deep breath. The two of us would be the very first contact that people had when they walked through the doors. I had to be strong. Falling apart, or succumbing to my own emotions, was not an option.

When the first applicants arrived, there was puzzlement. When they started to just walk to the first open computer station, we took them by the arm, or smiled invitingly, and walked with them to the open stations. One man looked at me and shook his head. "What *is* this? No one takes time like this to help people." I told him proudly that *we* did. And that we would. Throughout the duration of the program.

I smiled. I asked people's names. I told them my name. This was more than walking people through a line; we were now in the realm of building relationships. We were truly there to assist them in whatever ways we could.

I witnessed people wearing blankets around their shoulders, or cradling dogs in their arms, hearing repeatedly the stories of how these were the only things they had left in the world. They had lost their homes, their clothes and often their pets. All of the pictures and scrapbooks and family albums that had been passed down through their families for generations. Truly gut-wrenching experiences. One woman suddenly burst into tears and nearly fell to the floor sobbing as she walked in the doorway. I hugged her. "It wasn't real until right now," she shook with tears. "Until I got to this door, I could deny that any of this was happening. But... I can't. It really happened!"

So many people, so many faces, names, and stories. What touched me and truly carried me through, especially those first couple of days, was the attitude of gratitude. If anyone in the world had a right to be bitter, to feel unfriendly and uncaring, these were the people. Yet nearly every horrific story was underscored with the same sentiment: "But at least I'm still alive. It could be worse." The other prevalent sentiment was how thankful everyone was to "Miss Dolly." Miss Dolly was more than a celebrity here -- Miss Dolly was their patron saint. "Tell Miss Dolly we said thank you so much."

About an hour or so into the morning, a gentleman stood waiting his turn and shared his experience. "I lost everything, even my Bible. I met a guy out on the Parkway one day who was just handing them out, for free, and I asked him for one. He gave it to me and when I got home, I opened it up, looking for my favorite verses. And -- there stuck between the pages -- was a hundred dollar bill. How about that, huh?" He paused. "What happened to me was bad. It was real bad. But God has

just done so much already to help me. I'm
lucky, really. I've had a few people, all
strangers, just give me money when they
found out what had happened. I feel guilty. I
just know I need to share it." He produced a
biscuit wrapper from his jacket pocket. "I
stopped by Hardee's for a biscuit this morning
on my way here, and I thought, 'I can't stand
in that big line of people with a biscuit when
they don't have any.' So I just told the lady at
the window to give me 100 of them. And I…"

My mouth fell open. "You're the man
who was handing out biscuits in the line a
while ago! I thought it was someone who just
stopped by to be nice." I swallowed hard.
"You, my friend, are an amazing individual!
No wonder God keeps blessing you!"

It took less than four days for people to
start scamming. A certain slumlord kept being
called as individuals came in, to verify who
was living in the hotels at the time of the fires.
After three or four calls, he offered to make
them a list so they didn't have to keep calling.
How nice! Over the next few days, we learned
that he had made deals with associates: he
gave them the necessary information to claim
the $1000 checks, and, in return, he would

receive a mere $200 -- from each of them. Each of them would pocket an easy $800. But he would collect $200 each, from about thirty people, for six months.

The fallout was massive. A sign was posted, stating that anyone who lived at one of those two addresses would be refused a check. If there were questions, they should contact their landlord. Several people, upon reaching that point in the line, looked around sheepishly and left. The problem with this, however, was that there was the remote possibility that some legitimate residents had not yet gone through the line. No one really thought about that at the time, though; the important part was that the bad guys had been stopped.

On the final afternoon of month one, Cathy got food poisoning and left me to greet alone. The day was drawing to a close. My emotions were spent. The pain and suffering that I had encountered over those four days was truly palpable. I watched as a young lady, maybe twenty years old, stopped in front of that sign. She cocked her head and just kept looking at it, dazed. My first thought was that maybe she couldn't read, so I approached her with a smile and asked if I could help her. "I don't understand," she said. "I pre-registered online. I waited 'til the right day to come. What did I do wrong? I followed all the rules."

The team leaders had very plainly and succinctly told us no exceptions; send anyone from either of these addresses away. I looked from her to the empty stations inside. Should I follow my gut? "I can't promise anything, but let's see what we can do."

I greeted the intake volunteer quickly and quietly. "This young lady lives at one of the addresses on the signs."

My counterpart looked at me with widened eyes and stated that I would need to get one of the team leaders. So I stepped through the door and found one of them. I explained the situation. "Did you not understand, 'no exceptions?'"

"I did. But I think that she's legit."

A few moments later, after talking with the team leader, she left in tears. My heart sank. I just knew...

But a little while later, I looked up to see her again at the door. "This isn't about me," she said firmly. "I'm not here asking for money for me. *This is for my baby*!" she declared determinedly. I looked at the letter in her hands. Department of Welfare…

Again, I summoned a team leader. "I respectfully refuse to tell someone that she cannot come in here because of her address. If you want to be the one to do that, then you can."

Just then another team member, Laurel, stopped in her tracks. "What's going on?" I told her the situation. She pursed her lips and thanked me.

From the other side of the room, I held my breath, trying to read the situation as things played out. A couple of minutes later, Laurel walked by with my young friend. As she did, she said, "Come on, sweetheart. Let's go to the toy store we have set up to get that baby some Christmas presents. We'll give *them* a few minutes to do the right thing!"

Upon returning, they went back across the room. Excitedly, she hugged Laurel. She left tearfully. "She got it!"

I stood silently and bit my lip. It's an amazing feeling when you realize that you have served a specific purpose, completely humbling. I said my own prayer of thanks. If there was no other reason in the world for me to know so intuitively that I must be a part of the volunteer efforts here, then this was it. Someone else probably would have followed instructions. Someone else might have turned her away, regardless of her insistence. I tried to imagine what that must feel like. And I tried to be the kind of person who did the right thing. After all, these weren't just Dolly's people; they were my people, too.

Acknowledgements

As always, I begin my acknowledgements by thanking God for his blessings and gifts. I have more than I ever dreamed of, more than I ever deserved.

This collection of stories began coming together in my head in the Fall of 2018, too late in the year to market a Christmas collection, so I put them on a back burner and continued to write other things. Until I went to Denton Loving's amazing writer's retreat in May, The Orchard Keeper. I intended to work on a specific project while there, but once I arrived, I knew that the project had shifted and the Christmas stories started coming out on paper and electronically. This is not the first time that Denton's influence has shown up in my work. It was his wisdom that steered me in the direction of *Dog Days and Dragonflies* for the title of my first book, a fact that Margaret Atwood once told me I should be grateful for each and every day -- and I am!

So, once again, Denton, thank you for providing a place for writers to come to get away from the rest of the world to be with our thoughts, ideas, and find solace within the words we have within us, struggling to make their way out!

To my phenomenal husband, Russell Peters, words cannot begin to thank you for all the ways you support my writing, or even my other endeavors, with patience and nurturing like I've never known before you. Thank you for looking over pieces when I know that you were tired and even though you argued that you didn't know grammar rules, etc., and I argued back that I just needed a set of fresh eyes for context and logic. You have no idea how much those moments meant to me and how many times it kept me from completely giving up on a piece.

To my dear friend, colorist/stylist, Christy Blackburn, thank you for always encouraging me, for stocking my books in your shop, for fitting me in for last-minute "Chrissified" sessions on my hair, and most of all, just for being my friend. I still hold out hope for the day when we hit the big time and go on the road together so you can do my hair before each speaking engagement and earn a living that way!

To my roadtrip sidekick, Tasha Neel Hicks, let's make this our inspiration to get

Chasing After Rainbows onto paper, 'cos you know that I can't do it without you!

To my crazy friend Kandy Kiser Howlett, without whom I would have no GIF's and a llot less laughter in my life.

To my wonderful friend Becky Smith-Rangel, thanks for helping me get organized in other endeavors so I could try to get this book project tied up. I know that there were days when you were tired and would have much preferred to stay home and rest, but you came to the house to help me inventory Duran Duran stuff. For that reason and so many more, you are a saint! I love you dearly!

To Pam Smith Waddell, thank you for the many crazy nights from middle school throughout high school, where we watched videos and shared teen magazines, rented *Sing Blue Silver* and *The Lost Boys*, dreamed our dreams, schemed our schemes, and made the most of life in a small Southwestern Virginia town. I'm so glad to still call you friend after all these years. Here's to many, many more! (Roger is still yours!)

To all of my local post office staffs -- Downtown Bristol, Exit 5, Volunteer Parkway, and Blountville -- thanks for all that you do for me, and for keeping it real; a special thanks to Sandra for dealing with so many international packages, and to Anita, just because.

To Kyle and the Cracker Barrel Crew, I miss you guys! Thanks for giving me a special holiday season last year when I needed it more than I realized it, and for the employee discount that made Christmas a lot better for others, too.

To my Mary Kay Team, from Lyn Tatum down -- Beth Andis Fairbanks, Christie Kiser Davenport, Sharon Hall-Alderson, and Becky Smith-Rangel, specifically -- and those of you who were on my team at any given time (there are too many to try to mention at this point, so please forgive me). Thank you for the wonderful learning opportunities I had within that organization. Thank you for the support and encouragement, especially during that Christmas project with Heritage Hall. You helped me step out on faith, live by faith, and see it all through to grow by faith, as well.

To Chris White, a dear friend for many years, but a source of strength and true camaraderie in the past 15 months, after my mom's death. I appreciate you and your friendship, your wit and your wisdom, more than you will ever know.

To my friend Misty Yates (my furry children's godmother), thanks for always being there, whenever, and whatever I need you to do.

To Diana Olesen-Perkins, thanks for keeping me looking so smooth!

To my fabulously professional and deeply humane cohorts at the My People Fund, especially Christie Crouse, Angie Harris, and Kathy Brown, thanks for making an emotionally-taxing opportunity a blessing (and more fun than it probably should have been) each month for six months, and for the friendships that have endured since then. Thanks also to my sweet Tamara "Tam-Tam" Davis, for going with me to be part of the Team. Meeting Miss Dolly there beside you that day is something that I will never, ever forget. (Jebby loves you guys forever!)

To the staff at Northeast State Community College's Basler Library, thank you for logging me on as a guest (with printing privileges) for these past few months. You have helped me search, research, and have allowed me to bend your ears and bounce ideas off of you when I hit brick walls, or just got tired of writing or editing. Thanks for still treating me like family. Not all of my former work places would do that. A special thanks to Michelle Wyatt and to Virginia Salmon for their attention above and beyond to help me out, especially when I know that they had to be tired of me.

Also, to Virginia Salmon for once again being the fantabulous editor that she is! When I think that I cannot possibly look at the manuscript one more time, your edits encourage me to do that one more time, to get it done, to make it ready for the rest of the world to see. I absolutely cannot thank you enough!

For this book, I asked three long-time friends to do "initial" reads for me, just to sorta scan the material to see if it worked together okay cohesively. Thank you Heather Kingsford Bennett, Matthew Kingesly, and Susan Whittaker, for doing that. I love you guys!

Every book needs established authors to read and comment, give a general blurb about the material within that book, to let the general public know a little more about the book. My author blurbs for Blue Ridge Christmas came from some of the most talented authors I know, not all from my region. Many thanks to Rebecca Elswick (author of *Mama's Shoes*), Andrew "Durandy" Golub (author of *Beautiful Colors* and *The Music Between Us*), Denton Loving (author of *Crimes Against Birds*), and Karen Nolan (author of *Above the Fog*). Thank all of you for your kind words about *Blue Ridge Christmas*.

To Pat Shrader, for his continued support of my work, and technical assistance -- I will always need you!

To my wonderful mentor and friend Gretchen McCroskey, without whom I would never have begun submitting work to be published. And to Tamara Baxter, my first Creative Writing instructor at Northeast State, who taught me to be more concrete in my writing. Both of you ladies continue to serve as inspiration and role models for me!

To Lynne Bishop and Anna Buchanan Martin, I appreciate you guys so much. For everything. For ever.

To Shian Sparks for the amazing author photos that go on and on! And to Vickie Combs for the make-up and accessory assistance, for everything you've done to promote my work and just to believe in me over the years -- you know your business, Hoochie!

To Kimberley "Kimbo" Crawford, thanks for the crazy chaotic adventures -- here's to more!

To Sandra Childress, in the lowest of lows and darkest of darkness, thanks for remaining my friend and encouraging me to return to writing, knowing that it would bring me out to the light that was always there.

To Matthew Kingesly. I don't know that there is enough room to say everything that I need to say here. Matthew has guided this project since it started taking the form of a Christmas story collection. The title? His suggestion. The cover image? His suggestion. The marketing and PR strategies? His suggestions. Making me cut parts of the book that I thought were absolutely hilarious, but not necessarily needed? His suggestions. Not burning bridges that I didn't mean to burn? His insisted suggestions. I owe him so much gratitude that I honestly don't know where to begin, so I will simply say, "Thank you for being a friend."

To Tammy Mays Adams, thanks for always letting me crash, giving me wonderful tours, providing me with stories, for being my friend, and for trusting me with *our* pasts. I love you so much! Don't ever doubt your talents or worth! And now that it's official, thank you for the amazing book cover, too!

To Sandy Peters, a.k.a., "Mom," and Elise Peters, for always asking about my writing and about when my next book is coming out and always wanting to know what I'm writing about next, gently nudging me along, I thank you and appreciate you for never giving up and never losing hope that the light was still there for the past few years. It has meant more to me than words can express, so consider yourselves a huge part of the reason I've made it back.

To my friends and family, near and far -- my Duranie tribe, my high school friends, my college friends, my Facebook friends and followers -- to each and every person who has, at any time said that I could do this and supported or encouraged me/this project, I say thank you a hundred times over! Friends are hard to come by, and I am #Blessed!

To you, my readers, a great big thanks for reading, for buying, for supporting this book, however you have done so. If you have enjoyed this book, I hope that you will tell a friend. Or suggest that your local library buy a copy to add to their collection. As a self-published author, I depend largely on word of mouth publicity and reviews on online resources such as Good Reads and Amazon. If you can take a few minutes to leave a few nice words there, it goes a long way towards helping the success of any author, but especially those of us out here trying to make it work on our own.

About the Author & Book Cover Artist

The Author:

Chrissie Anderson Peters grew up in Tazewell, Virginia, and has lived just across the state line in Bristol, Tennessee, since 2000. She resides with her husband Russ and their 7 feline children. She holds a BA in English/Education from Emory & Henry College, and a Masters of Science in Information Sciences from The University of Tennessee, Knoxville. Her passions include traveling, 80's music, and writing. *Blue Ridge Christmas* is her third self-published book; her first two were *Dog Days and Dragonflies* (2012), and *Running From Crazy* (2013), both available through Amazon.com and BN.com

The Book Cover Artist:

Tammy Mays Adams resides in New Orleans with her husband of 27 years, Jason, 10 year old son, Samuel, and sweet fur babies. Tammy's heart never waivers far from the Appalachian Mountains, where she was born, raised, and educated. She has an Associates in Arts and Science Degree from Southwest

Virginia Community College, and a Bachelor
of Arts degree from Virginia Intermont
College. Tammy works with all media of art,
her favorite being photography. However, she
is inspired by all art, all beauty, and all types
of artists. Jesus gives her the ability to create.
Tammy also enjoys music festivals, globe
trotting, spending time with loved ones, and is
a foodie.